Introducing "Cooking Fun for Kids," an easy recipe cookbook designed specifically for young aspiring chefs. This cookbook is filled with simple and delicious recipes that are easy to follow and perfect for children of all ages.

The book contains a wide variety of recipes, ranging from breakfast dishes to tasty snacks and desserts. Each recipe is accompanied by step-by-step instructions that are written in a clear and concise language, making it easy for kids to follow along. The book also features colorful illustrations that make the recipes come to life and will inspire children to get creative in the kitchen.

In addition to the recipes, "Cooking Fun for Kids" also includes helpful tips and tricks for young cooks. These tips cover everything from basic kitchen safety to how to properly measure ingredients. This cookbook is a great way to introduce children to the joys of cooking, while also teaching them valuable life skills that will stay with them for years to come.

Whether your child is a beginner in the kitchen or a seasoned pro, "Cooking Fun for Kids" is the perfect cookbook to help them develop their culinary skills and creativity. With its easy-to-follow recipes and fun illustrations, this cookbook is sure to become a favorite in any household with young chefs.

Bean Burritos

Here's a list of ingredients for making bean burritos:

1 can (16 ounces) vegetarian refried beans
1 cup salsa
1 cup cooked long grain rice
2 cups shredded cheddar cheese, divided
12 flour tortillas (6 inches)
Shredded lettuce (optional)

Instructions:

Preheat the oven to 350°F (175°C).

In a large bowl, mix together the refried beans and salsa.

Spread a spoonful of the bean mixture down the center of each tortilla.

Sprinkle a few tablespoons of cooked rice over the bean mixture, followed by a handful of shredded cheese.

Roll up the tortilla to enclose the filling, and place the burritos seam-side down in a large baking dish.

Sprinkle the remaining cheese over the top of the burritos.

Bake for 20-25 minutes, or until the cheese is melted and the burritos are heated through.

Serve the burritos hot, topped with shredded lettuce, if desired. Enjoy!

Chicken Fried Rice

Chicken Fried Rice is a delicious, easy and fast meal that you can prepare in minutes. It's one of the most popular chicken recipes around, and it's easy to see why! This comfort food dish packs plenty of flavor and nutrition all into one easy-to-make meal.

The ingredients in Chicken Fried Rice are simple, but the flavors are anything but. Start by heating oil (both sesame and vegetable) in a wok or large skillet over medium-high heat. Once hot, add chicken breasts and sauté until cooked through. Add frozen peas and carrots, green onions, garlic, eggs and cooked rice to the pan and cook until everything is heated through. Finally, stir in low-sodium soy sauce for some added flavor and serve.

With just a few simple ingredients and easy steps, you can have a delicious meal ready to go in no time! So next time you're looking for an easy and flavorful chicken recipe, give Chicken Fried Rice a try - it's sure to be a hit!

Happy cooking!

Creamy Mushroom Pasta

Ingredients

8 ounces fettuccine pasta.
2 tablespoons olive oil.
¾ pound fresh white mushrooms, sliced.
¼ pound fresh shiitake mushrooms, stemmed and sliced.
salt and ground black pepper to taste.
2 cloves garlic, minced.
2 fluid ounces sherry.
1 cup chicken stock.

If you're looking for delicious recipes for kids, this creamy mushroom pasta is sure to please. With just a few ingredients and some simple steps, you can have an amazing dinner on your table in no time!

To start, bring a large pot of lightly salted water to a boil over high heat. Add the fettuccine pasta and cook for 8 to 10 minutes, or until al dente. Drain the pasta and set aside.

Next, heat the olive oil in a large skillet over medium-high heat. Add the mushrooms, season with salt and pepper, and sauté for 5 minutes. Reduce the heat to low, add the garlic and sherry, and cook for another 2 minutes.

Finally, add the chicken stock and bring to a boil. Once boiling, reduce heat to low and simmer for 5 minutes. Add the cooked fettuccine pasta and stir until the sauce coats the noodles evenly. Serve warm and enjoy!

This delicious mushroom pasta is sure to be a hit with kids of all ages. With its creamy sauce and delicious mushrooms, it's sure to become a family favorite. So don't wait any longer - try this delicious recipe today!

Bon Appétit!

Arugula Pizza

INGREDIENTS

1 ¼ cup pizza sauce (purchased or our favorite Easy Pizza Sauce)
1 cup (3 ounces) shredded smoked gouda cheese.
½ cup shredded Parmesan cheese.
6 ounces fresh mozzarella cheese.
4 cups (3 ounces) baby arugula.
1 tablespoon extra virgin olive oil.
¼ teaspoon kosher salt, plus more for sprinkling.

If you're looking for delicious pizza recipes, look no further than this delicious arugula pizza. This delicious and easy-to-prepare meal is perfect for any day of the week. To make it, start by preheating your oven to 500°F (260°C). Next, spread 1 ¼ cups of purchased or homemade pizza sauce on a 12 inch baking sheet lined with parchment paper. Top with 1 cup (3 ounces) shredded smoked gouda cheese, ½ cup shredded Parmesan cheese, and 6 ounces fresh mozzarella cheese. Bake in the preheated oven for 10 minutes until golden brown and bubbly. Once done baking, top the pizza with 4 cups (3 ounces) baby arugula and sprinkle with 1 tablespoon extra virgin olive oil and ¼ teaspoon kosher salt. Slice, serve, and enjoy! With its delicious combination of flavors, this delicious arugula pizza is sure to become a family favorite. Enjoy!

Air Fryer Chicken Meatballs

Into a large mixing bowl, add ground chicken, egg, bread crumbs, parmesan cheese, salt, pepper, garlic powder, onion powder, paprika, olive oil and parsley and mix until combined. No, take a heaping tablespoon from the chicken mixture and shape it into a ball.

Next, place the chicken meatballs in the air fryer basket and set to 375°F for 12-15 minutes flipping halfway through. This healthy recipe is an easy and fast way to make delicious, low budget meals! You can top these chicken meatballs over pasta or a salad for a complete meal. With air frying, you don't have to worry about the oil or the mess. No need to stand over a hot stove, just preheat and enjoy healthy eating in no time! You can also try this recipe with ground turkey or beef for even more delicious variations. Air frying has revolutionized healthy cooking; easy, fast and healthy recipes are now achievable at home without sacrificing taste. Try this easy air fryer chicken meatballs recipe and enjoy healthy eating today!

The end result: delicious, healthy air fryer chicken meatballs that are an easy and fast way to make low budget meals. With just a few ingredients and the air fryer, you can have healthy meals on the table in no time. Enjoy!

Chicken Alfredo

Ingredients

1 tbsp olive oil.
4 skinless boneless chicken thighs, cut in half.
300g fettuccine, or tagliatelle.
1 tbsp butter.
200ml double cream.
½ a nutmeg, grated.
100g parmesan.
parsley, chopped, to serve.

This easy and fast chicken alfredo recipe is the perfect midweek meal. It only takes around 30 minutes to prepare and cook, so you can have a delicious dinner on the table in no time.

To make this dish, start by heating the olive oil in a large frying pan over medium-high heat. Once hot, add the chicken thighs and cook for 5 minutes on each side until golden.
Next, cook the fettuccine according to packet instructions.

Meanwhile, in a separate saucepan, melt butter over medium heat. Add cream, nutmeg and parmesan to the pan and bring to a gentle simmer. Stir occasionally for around 10 minutes until the sauce is thick and creamy.

Once your chicken and pasta are cooked, add them to the cream sauce and stir to combine.
Serve with a sprinkle of chopped parsley for extra flavour. Enjoy!

Tuna Pasta

Ingredients

2 tablespoons olive oil.
2 large cloves garlic minced.
1 (5 ounce) can tuna, drained I prefer tuna packed in oil.
1 teaspoon lemon juice.
1 tablespoon fresh parsley chopped.
Salt & pepper to taste.
4 ounces uncooked pasta (I used spaghetti)

Tuna pasta is a delicious and easy-to-make recipe for kids. It's perfect for busy weeknights when you don't have much time to cook. To make this delicious dish, start by heating the olive oil in a large skillet over medium heat. Add the garlic and sauté until fragrant, about 1 minute. Add the tuna and stir to combine. Then add the lemon juice and parsley, season with salt and pepper to taste, and cook for another minute or two. Finally, add the uncooked pasta to the skillet and mix everything together. Cook according to directions on the box until al dente. Serve hot and enjoy! Tuna pasta is a delicious and nutritious meal that your kids will love. Enjoy!

Baked Fish

Here's a list of ingredients for a baked fish recipe:

White fish fillets
Cherry tomatoes
Red onion
Garlic
Green olives
Capers
Fresh parsley
Olive oil
Dried oregano
Lemon juice
Salt and pepper, to taste

Instructions:

Preheat the oven to 375°F (190°C).

Line a baking dish with parchment paper or lightly grease it with oil.

Rinse the fish fillets and pat them dry with paper towels. Place them in the prepared baking dish.

Slice the cherry tomatoes in half and arrange them around the fish fillets.

Thinly slice the red onion and scatter it over the tomatoes.

Mince the garlic and sprinkle it over the onions.

Add the green olives and capers to the dish.

Chop the fresh parsley and sprinkle it over the top of the fish.

Drizzle the dish with olive oil and sprinkle with dried oregano.

Squeeze the lemon juice over the dish and season with salt and pepper, to taste.

Bake the fish in the preheated oven for 20-25 minutes, or until the fish is opaque and flakes easily with a fork.

Serve the baked fish hot, garnished with additional chopped parsley, if desired. Enjoy!

Healthy Salmon Pasta

Ingredients

8 ounces spaghetti or other pasta, uncooked
1/2 pound fresh salmon
1/4 teaspoon onion powder
Salt & pepper, to taste
1 tablespoon olive oil
1 tablespoon butter
1 tablespoon flour
3 cloves garlic, minced

Instructions for preparing Healthy Salmon Pasta:

Cook the spaghetti or other pasta according to the package directions. Reserve 1/2 cup of the pasta cooking water and drain the rest.

Cut the salmon into 1-inch pieces and season with onion powder, salt, and pepper.

In a large skillet, heat the olive oil over medium heat. Add the seasoned salmon and cook until just browned on the outside, about 2-3 minutes per side. Remove the salmon from the skillet and set aside.

In the same skillet, melt the butter over medium heat. Whisk in the flour until smooth and cook for 1 minute, or until the mixture starts to turn golden brown.

Stir in the minced garlic and cook for an additional minute, or until fragrant. Gradually whisk in the reserved pasta cooking water until the sauce is smooth.

Add the cooked salmon back into the skillet and stir to coat with the sauce. Cook for 2-3 minutes, or until the salmon is cooked through.

Toss the cooked pasta with the salmon sauce in the skillet. Serve immediately, garnished with chopped parsley or other herbs, if desired.

Enjoy your delicious and healthy Salmon Pasta!

Potato Soup

Ingredients

8 slices thin bacon, cut into 1-inch pieces
1 medium onion, diced
2 medium carrots, scrubbed clean and diced
2 stalks celery, diced
4 small russet potatoes, peeled and diced
8 cups low-sodium chicken or vegetable broth
3 tablespoons all-purpose flour
1 cup milk

Instructions for preparing Potato Soup:

In a large pot, cook the bacon over medium heat until crispy, about 5-7 minutes. Remove the bacon with a slotted spoon and set aside. Reserve 2 tablespoons of the bacon fat in the pot.

Add the diced onion, carrots, and celery to the pot and cook until the vegetables are soft and the onion is translucent, about 5-7 minutes.

Stir in the diced potatoes and the chicken or vegetable broth. Bring the soup to a boil, then reduce the heat and simmer until the potatoes are tender, about 20-25 minutes.

In a separate bowl, whisk together the flour and milk until smooth. Stir the flour mixture into the soup and cook until the soup has thickened, about 5-7 minutes.

Return the cooked bacon to the pot and stir to combine. Season the soup with salt and pepper, to taste.

Serve the soup hot, garnished with freshly chopped parsley or green onions, if desired.

Enjoy your delicious and comforting Potato Soup!

Baked Feta Pasta

ingredients

2 pints (20 oz) grape tomatoes.
1/2 cup extra-virgin olive oil.
Salt and freshly ground black pepper.
7 oz. block feta cheese (sheep's milk variety), drained.
10 oz. dry pasta (bite size)
5 medium garlic cloves, peeled and halved.
8 oz. ...
1/4 tsp crushed red pepper flakes, or more to taste.

Baked Feta Pasta is an easy and healthy dish that takes only minimal time to prepare. With just a handful of simple ingredients, you can create this delicious meal. To make it, start by preheating your oven to 425 degrees Fahrenheit.

In a large bowl, combine the grape tomatoes, extra-virgin olive oil, salt and pepper. Cut the feta cheese into small cubes and add it to the bowl. Next, cook 10 oz of bite-size pasta according to package instructions until al dente. Once done, drain it and mix it with the tomato mixture in the bowl.

Add garlic cloves, 8 oz of mushrooms (sliced), and 1/4 tsp of crushed red pepper flakes, or to taste. Toss everything together and spread it in a single layer on an oven-safe dish. Bake for 25 minutes until the top is lightly golden brown.

Baked Feta Pasta is now ready to enjoy! Serve with a sprinkling of fresh herbs, extra olive oil, and a side of crusty bread. This healthy pasta dish makes for a great weeknight dinner that is sure to please the whole family. Enjoy!

Chicken Noodle Casserole

Ingredients
12 oz. wide egg noodles.
10.5-oz. cans cream of chicken soup.
1 c. whole milk.
1 c. shredded sharp cheddar cheese.
1 tsp. ground black pepper.
1/2 tsp. kosher salt.
3 c. cooked, shredded chicken (from 1 rotisserie chicken)
1/2. small yellow onion, finely chopped.

Making a chicken noodle casserole is an easy and healthy dinner option for kids. To begin, preheat your oven to 400 degrees Fahrenheit. In a large pot over medium heat, cook the egg noodles according to package directions. Drain the cooked noodles and set aside.

In a medium-sized bowl, combine the cream of chicken soup, milk, shredded cheese, ground black pepper and kosher salt. Stir until the ingredients are completely blended.

In a 9-by-13-inch baking dish, spread the cooked egg noodles. Top with the shredded chicken and onion pieces. Pour the cream of chicken mixture over the noodles and chicken, spreading evenly to ensure everything is coated.

Bake for 25 minutes until the cheese is melted and bubbly. Let cool for about 10 minutes before serving. Enjoy!

This chicken noodle casserole provides a comforting, delicious and healthy dinner option for kids. It's quick to prepare, full of flavor and sure to please everyone at the table.

Nacho Pie

Ingredients

4 cups nacho tortilla chips, coarsely crushed.
1 pound ground beef.
1/2 cup chopped onion.
1 can (16 ounces) chili beans, undrained, warmed.
1 can (8 ounces) tomato sauce.
1 cup shredded part-skim mozzarella cheese.

Preheat your oven to 350°F (180°C).

In a large skillet, cook ground beef and onion over medium heat until browned. Drain any excess fat.

Stir in the warmed chili beans, tomato sauce, and 2 cups of the crushed tortilla chips. Cook for about 5 minutes, stirring occasionally.

Grease a 9-inch (23 cm) pie dish and spread the remaining 2 cups of crushed tortilla chips evenly on the bottom of the dish.

Pour the beef mixture over the tortilla chips, spreading it evenly.

Sprinkle the shredded mozzarella cheese over the beef mixture.

Bake in the preheated oven for 20-25 minutes, or until cheese is melted and bubbly.

Let the nacho pie cool for a few minutes before serving. Enjoy!

Pesto Pasta

Ingredients

6 ounces spaghetti, reserve 1/2 cup starchy pasta water.
1/3 to 1/2 cup. basil pesto or vegan pesto.
Extra-virgin olive oil, for drizzling.
Fresh lemon juice, as desired.
4 cups arugula.
2 tablespoons pine nuts.
Pinches of red pepper flakes.
Sea salt and freshly ground black pepper.

Cooking delicious recipes for kids doesn't have to be complicated. With the right ingredients, you can make delicious pesto pasta in a flash! To begin, bring a large pot of salted water to a boil and add the spaghetti. Cook according to package instructions until al dente. Reserve 1/2 cup of starchy pasta water before straining.

In a large bowl, mix together the basil pesto, arugula and pine nuts and season with salt, pepper and red pepper flakes to taste. Next, add the cooked spaghetti to the pesto mixture along with a little of the reserved pasta water to thin out the sauce if desired. Drizzle with extra-virgin olive oil and lemon juice, if desired.

Give the delicious pesto pasta a good stir to coat all the ingredients evenly. Plate up and enjoy! This delicious recipe is sure to be a hit with kids of all ages and tastes great as leftovers too. Give it a try today and enjoy some delicious pesto pasta for dinner tonight!

Happy cooking!

Garlic Parmesan Sweet Potato Wedges

Garlic Parmesan Sweet Potato Wedges are a delicious and healthy lunch option for kids! These wedges are packed with flavor, thanks to the combination of grated Parmesan cheese, garlic powder, dried parsley and oregano, as well as paprika. Best of all, they're made with just four simple ingredients - sweet potatoes, eggs, Parmesan cheese and salt. To prepare them, simply preheat your oven to 400 degrees F. Cut the sweet potatoes into wedges and place onto a lightly greased baking sheet. In a small bowl, beat together the egg and Parmesan cheese until combined. Pour this mixture over the wedges and sprinkle with salt, pepper, garlic powder, dried parsley, oregano and paprika. Bake for 25 minutes or until the wedges are golden brown. Serve them with your favorite dip or as is - they're sure to become a family favorite! Enjoy!

- Garlic Parmesan Sweet Potato Wedges are a great way to sneak in some extra veggies into your kids' lunch!
- Get creative with the seasonings - feel free to add more of your favorite herbs and spices for an extra kick of flavor.
- These wedges also make a great side dish or snack - they're sure to be a hit at any gathering!
- Try adding Parmesan cheese to the top of the wedges near the end of cooking for extra cheesy goodness. Enjoy!

- Make sure to use freshly grated Parmesan cheese for best results - pre-shredded Parmesan will not melt and blend as well as fresh.
- These wedges pair perfectly with ketchup, mustard, ranch dip or your favorite sauce!
- Feel free to add chopped fresh parsley or oregano for an extra pop of freshness.
- Make sure to watch the wedges closely at the end of cooking - they can burn quickly if left in the oven too long. Enjoy!

Pasta Salad

Ingredients
- 1 pound tri-colored spiral pasta. Great Value ROTINI, 16OZ.
- 1 (16 ounce) bottle Italian-style salad dressing.
- 6 tablespoons salad seasoning mix.
- 2 cups cherry tomatoes, diced.
- 1 green bell pepper, chopped.
- 1 red bell pepper, diced.
- ½ yellow bell pepper, chopped.
- 1 (2.25 ounce) can black olives, chopped.

Pasta salad is a classic lunch time favorite and this recipe will be sure to please the entire family! With its colorful vegetables, an Italian-style dressing, and tri-colored spiral pasta, you can make a healthy, delicious meal in no time.

To make the pasta salad, start by cooking one pound of tri-colored spiral pasta according to package instructions. Once cooked, drain the pasta and set aside.

In a separate bowl, mix together one (16-ounce) bottle of Italian-style salad dressing with 6 tablespoons of salad seasoning mix until completely combined.

Next, add in 2 cups of diced cherry tomatoes, 1 chopped green bell pepper, 1 diced red bell pepper, and 1/2 chopped yellow bell pepper. Lastly, stir in one (2.25-ounce) can of black olives that have been chopped.

Now combine the cooked pasta with the vegetable mixture and pour the Italian dressing over top. Gently mix everything together until everything is evenly coated. Serve chilled or at room temperature for a light and healthy lunch. Enjoy!

Pasta salad is a great way to get your kids to eat their vegetables, and this recipe will have them asking for more! Try making it today for an easy and delicious meal that the whole family can enjoy. Bon appetit!

Creamy Tomato Soup

Tomato Soup is a great lunch choice for kids because it's easy to make and packed with healthy ingredients. Plus, they will love the bright and vibrant colour! Here's what you'll need to make this delicious tomato soup recipe:

- 1-1.25kg/2lb 4oz-2lb 12oz ripe tomatoes

- 1 medium onion

- 1 small carrot

- 1 celery stick

- 2 tbsp olive oil

- 2 squirts of tomato purée (about 2 tsp)

- A good pinch of sugar

- 2 bay leaves

Once you've gathered all the ingredients, it's time to start cooking! Begin by heating the olive oil in a large saucepan and adding the diced onion, carrot, celery stick. Cook over medium heat for about 5 minutes until softened. Then add the tomatoes, purée, bay leaves and sugar. Cover with a lid and cook for 40 minutes. Once the soup is cooked, remove the bay leaves and blend until smooth with a blender.

Serve up this delicious tomato soup with some crusty bread or croutons on top and you have an easy, healthy lunch that your kids will love! Enjoy!

Spinach And Feta Pizza

Ingredients

2 large Pizza Bases (see notes)
½ cup Tomato Paste.
½ Brown / Yellow Onion, finely diced.
½ Red Capsicum / Bell Pepper, finely diced.
100g / 3.5 oz Baby Spinach, roughly chopped.
4 White Mushrooms, thinly sliced.
½ cup Feta Cheese, crumbled.
1 ½ cups Shredded Mozzarella Cheese (or more, to taste)

Making delicious spinach and feta pizzas is easy and delicious. To begin, preheat your oven to 200°C / 392°F. Place the pizza bases on a lightly greased baking tray. Spread a thin layer of tomato paste over each base, then scatter the diced onion, capsicum / bell pepper, mushrooms, baby spinach and crumbled feta cheese over the top. Sprinkle with mozzarella cheese (you can add more if desired). Bake for 15-20 minutes or until golden brown and bubbly. Serve hot! Enjoy your delicious spinach and feta pizza!

These delicious spinach and feta pizzas are sure to become a family favorite in no time! The combination of flavors from the vegetables, feta and mozzarella cheese makes for a delicious meal that is sure to please everyone. With just a few simple ingredients, you can easily make delicious pizza recipes at home with ease! No need to order take-out anymore - now you can make delicious pizzas right in your own kitchen. Enjoy!

Shrimps Alfredo Pasta

Shrimp Alfredo pasta is a delicious and easy recipe to make for kids. It's quick, delicious, and full of flavor! To start, you'll need to gather all the necessary ingredients: Fettuccine pasta, shrimp (I used frozen raw 31-40 count per pound size shrimp; you can use smaller or larger), butter (unsalted), cream cheese (for added texture and tangy taste), heavy cream, chicken broth (for added flavor), garlic, and Parmesan cheese.

Once you have all of the ingredients ready to go, start by cooking the fettuccine pasta according to package instructions. Once cooked, drain and set aside. In a large skillet or pan, heat butter over medium-high heat. Add the shrimp to the skillet and cook for 3-5 minutes or until they turn pink. Next, add in the garlic and sauté for 2 minutes. Add in cream cheese, heavy cream, and chicken broth and mix everything together until well combined. Lastly, add in the cooked fettuccine pasta and stir for 1-2 minutes until everything is well incorporated. Serve the delicious Shrimp Alfredo pasta with a generous helping of freshly grated Parmesan cheese. Enjoy!

This delicious Shrimp Alfredo pasta recipe is sure to please the whole family, kids included! It's an easy and delicious way to show your family how much you care. Plus, it's a great way to teach kids how to cook delicious recipes for themselves. So what are you waiting for? Give this delicious Shrimp Alfredo pasta recipe a try today!

Chicken Quesadillas

Ingredients

1 pound skinless, boneless chicken breast, diced.
1 (1.27 ounce) packet fajita seasoning.
1 tablespoon vegetable oil.
2 green bell peppers, chopped.
2 red bell peppers, chopped.
1 onion, chopped. ...
10 (10 inch) flour tortillas.
1 (8 ounce) package shredded Cheddar cheese.

Chicken quesadillas make for a healthy and easy dinner for the whole family. To start preparing, dice the boneless chicken breasts and season with fajita seasoning. In a large skillet over medium heat, heat vegetable oil and add in the diced chicken breast, green bell peppers, red bell peppers, and onions. Cook until vegetables are softened and chicken is cooked through. To assemble the quesadillas, place about ¼ cup of cheese onto one side of a tortilla. Top with cooked vegetables and chicken, then add another ¼ cup of cheese to the top. Fold over into a half-moon shape and cook in a skillet on medium-high heat until golden brown. Repeat this process with the remaining tortillas. Serve warm and enjoy!

For a fun variation, try adding black beans to the quesadillas or swapping out Cheddar cheese for Monterey Jack. Using flavorful ingredients like jalapenos, salsa, and guacamole can also liven up this classic dish. Chicken quesadillas make for a healthy and delicious dinner that can be customized to fit the tastes of any family. Enjoy!

Salmon Burger

Ingredients

1½ pounds skinless, boneless salmon.
2 teaspoons Dijon mustard.
2 shallots, peeled and cut into chunks.
½ cup coarse bread crumbs.
1 tablespoon capers, drained.
Salt and black pepper.
2 tablespoons butter or olive oil.
Lemon wedges.

With all the necessary ingredients in hand, you can easily prepare a nutritious and delicious salmon burger lunch for your kids. Begin by preheating the oven to 350 degrees Fahrenheit. Then place the salmon in a food processor and process until it becomes somewhat smooth. Add mustard, shallots, bread crumbs, capers, salt, and pepper, and process until everything is combined.

Form the mixture into four patties and place on a greased baking sheet. Bake in preheated oven for 20 minutes, flipping the burgers halfway through cooking time. When done, remove from oven and heat butter or oil in a large skillet over medium heat. Place salmon burgers in skillet cook for 3 to 4 minutes per side. Serve with a lemon wedge, and enjoy! The perfect healthy lunch recipe for kids!

This salmon burger recipe is sure to please even the pickiest eaters. Not only is it delicious, but it's also a great way to incorporate nutrient-rich fish into your family's meals. With just a few simple steps, you can easily prepare a nutritious and filling lunch in no time! Try this salmon burger recipe today and enjoy the deliciousness.

Chicken Avocado Rolls

Ingredients

1 cup cooked chicken breast diced or shredded.
1 avocado. pitted and diced.
1/4 cup shredded cheese or choice.
1/4 cup diced tomato.
2 tablespoons onion minced (optional)
2 tablespoons cilantro minced.
2 tablespoons sour-cream or Greek yogurt.
1 tablespoon lime juice.

Chicken avocado rolls are the perfect healthy lunch option for your kids. With only a few simple ingredients, you can easily put together this delicious and nutritious meal in no time! Start with 1 cup of cooked chicken breast diced or shredded. Then add one diced avocado, 1/4 cup of shredded cheese (or whatever type you prefer), 1/4 cup of diced tomato, 2 tablespoons of minced onion (optional), 2 tablespoons of minced cilantro, 2 tablespoons of sour-cream or Greek yogurt and 1 tablespoon of lime juice. Mix it all together and spoon the mixture into some lettuce leaves to make your chicken avocado rolls! Serve them up with a side salad or some steamed veggies for extra nutrition. Your kids will love them!

Easy Chicken Salad

INGREDIENTS
3 CUPS COOKED CHICKEN, DICED,
(I LIKE TO USE ROTISSERIE CHICKEN)
1/2 CUP MAYONNAISE.
1/2 CUP FINELY CHOPPED CELERY.
1/3 CUP SLICED GREEN ONIONS.
2 TEASPOONS LEMON JUICE.
1/2 TEASPOON KOSHER SALT,
(MORE TO TASTE)

To make easy chicken salad, start by combining the diced cooked chicken, mayonnaise, celery, green onions, lemon juice and salt together in a large bowl. Stir the ingredients until everything is evenly mixed. Taste and adjust seasonings as desired. Serve this delicious chicken salad with crackers or bread for lunch or dinner. It's also great for making sandwiches or wraps. Enjoy!

For a variation, you can add in some of your favorite ingredients like chopped olives, diced apples, dried cranberries, shredded cheese or even grapes. Get creative and make this easy chicken salad unique to your own taste! This is also a great way to use up any leftover cooked chicken you have. If you're looking for a healthier version, try substituting Greek yogurt for the mayonnaise and adding lots of fresh herbs. Enjoy!

This easy chicken salad is a great dish to add to your menu rotation. It's quick, delicious and versatile. Plus, it's sure to be a hit with the whole family. Serve it with your favorite sides for an easy and tasty lunch or dinner! Enjoy!

Chicken Noddle Soup

Ingredients
- 2 tablespoons unsalted butter.
- 1 onion, diced.
- 2 carrots, peeled and diced.
- 2 celery ribs, diced.
- 3 cloves garlic, minced.
- 8 cups chicken stock.
- 2 bay leaves.
- Kosher salt freshly ground black pepper, to taste.

This chicken noodle soup is a classic, healthy lunch recipe for kids. It's an easy-to-prepare dish that's both nourishing and delicious! Start by melting the butter in a large pot or Dutch oven over medium heat. Add the onions, carrots and celery to the pot and cook until softened, about 5 minutes. Add the garlic and cook for an additional minute. Pour in the chicken stock and add the bay leaves, season with salt and pepper to taste. Bring to a boil then reduce heat to low and simmer for 10-15 minutes until vegetables are tender. Finally, add the noodles of your choice - such as egg noodles or spiralized zucchini - and cook until noodles are al dente. Serve hot with your favorite toppings, like shredded cheese or fresh herbs. You can also refrigerate any leftovers for up to four days or freeze it for up to three months. Enjoy!

Tofu Sandwich

Are you looking for vegetarian recipes for kids? Then look no further than this delicious tofu sandwich. It's a healthy and easy meal that your children will adore. Start by toasting some of their favorite bread, and spread with Thousand Island dressing. To make the sandwich extra special, add lettuce, tomatoes, avocado, cucumber and sprouts. This vegetarian recipe is sure to please everyone in the family! To prepare it, simply assemble all of the ingredients into the sandwich and serve. Your kids will love it! Enjoy!

The tofu sandwich is a great vegetarian alternative for kids and makes a healthy, easy meal that can be prepared quickly. A delicious combination of toasted bread, Thousand Island dressing, lettuce, tomatoes, avocado, cucumber and sprouts makes this vegetarian recipe both nutritious and tasty. It's an ideal way to get your kids to enjoy vegetarian meals - just assemble the ingredients into the sandwich and serve! Your children will love it and you can feel good knowing they are getting their daily dose of veggies. Kids need all the nutrition they can get - so why not try this vegetarian recipe today? Enjoy!

Broccoli Shrimp Alfredo

Ingredients

1 16-ounce packages fettuccine.
1 pound uncooked medium shrimp, peeled and deveined.
3 garlic cloves, minced.
½ cup butter, cubed.
1 8-ounce packages cream cheese, cubed.
1 cup milk.
½ cup shredded Parmesan cheese.
6 cups frozen broccoli florets.

Instructions:

Cook the fettuccine according to the package instructions until al dente. Drain and set aside.

In a large skillet or saucepan, heat some oil over medium heat. Add the minced garlic and cook for 30 seconds until fragrant.

Add the uncooked shrimp to the skillet and cook until pink and cooked through, about 2-3 minutes. Remove the shrimp from the skillet and set aside.

In the same skillet, melt the butter over medium heat. Stir in the cream cheese until melted and smooth.

Gradually add the milk to the skillet, whisking constantly, until the sauce is smooth and creamy. Stir in the shredded Parmesan cheese until melted and well combined.

Stir in the cooked fettuccine, cooked shrimp, and frozen broccoli florets into the sauce until well combined.

Cook the broccoli shrimp alfredo until the broccoli is tender and heated through, about 3-5 minutes.

Serve the broccoli shrimp alfredo hot, garnished with additional Parmesan cheese and fresh herbs if desired.

Enjoy your delicious and creamy broccoli shrimp alfredo!

Greek Salad

Greek salad is the perfect healthy lunch for your kids! It's packed with fresh, nutrient-rich veggies like cucumbers, tomatoes, green bell pepper, red onion and olives. Adding a few slices of feta cheese will give it a creamy flavor and some extra calcium for added nutrition. For an even fresher touch, I like to add a handful of mint leaves. Your kids will love the flavorful combination and you can rest assured knowing they are getting a healthy meal. Enjoy!

Bonus tip: Use balsamic vinegar or lemon juice as a delicious dressing instead of using oil to make it extra light and nutritious.

I hope you enjoyed this healthy lunch recipe idea for your kids. Try it out today and let me know what you think!
Happy eating!

Chicken Tacos

Ingredients

¼ cup olive oil.
2 medium yellow onions, finely chopped.
2 bell peppers (any color), finely chopped.
4 cloves garlic, finely chopped.
2 pounds ground chicken (not extra-lean all breast meat)
1 tablespoon paprika.
2 teaspoons ancho chili powder.
1½ teaspoons ground cumin.

Preparing chicken tacos is a healthy and easy dinner option that kids will love. To make them, begin by heating ¼ cup of olive oil in a large skillet over medium-high heat. Add in chopped onions and bell peppers, as well as the minced garlic, stirring everything until it's lightly browned and fragrant.

Then, add in the ground chicken, breaking it up with a spoon as you stir. Once the chicken is cooked through, sprinkle in paprika, ancho chili powder and cumin. Stir everything to combine and let it cook for 3-4 minutes until all of the flavors have melded together.

Once done, serve your chicken tacos with tortillas, your favorite toppings and a side dish. Enjoy!

This is an easy yet tasty way to whip up a healthy dinner for the kids!

By following these easy steps, you can have a delicious batch of chicken tacos ready in no time. Not only are they healthy and delicious, but your kids will love them too! Try it out today for a quick and tasty dinner option.

Enjoy!

Vegetable Pizza

Vegetarian pizza is a flavorful and healthy option for kids that's simple to prepare. There are so many vegetarian pizza toppings available, it's easy to create unique recipes that appeal to the whole family.

To make vegetarian pizza, start by preheating your oven according to the instructions on the package of store-bought or homemade pizza dough. Next, select your favorite vegetarian toppings. Tomatoes, onions, arugula, kale, eggplants, bell peppers, spinach, zucchini and mushrooms all make wonderful vegetarian topping choices. For even more flavor you can add in some cooked or roasted vegetables such as olives or artichoke hearts. Spread your selected toppings over the prepared crust and top with your desired amount of cheese.

Bake the vegetarian pizza in the oven according to the dough packaging instructions and enjoy! Vegetarian pizzas are a great way to provide kids with healthy vegetarian recipes that they can enjoy. Experiment with different types of vegetables, cheeses and seasonings to create vegetarian recipes for kids that everyone will love. With just a few simple steps you can have a delicious vegetarian pizza ready to eat in no time!

Roasted Black Bean Burger

Ingredients

1½ red onions.
200 g mixed mushrooms.
100 g rye bread.
ground coriander.
1 x 400 g tin of black beans.
40 g mature Cheddar cheese.
4 soft rolls.
100 g ripe cherry tomatoes.

Instructions

Preheat the oven to 200°C (180°C fan) / 400°F / Gas Mark 6. Line a baking sheet with parchment paper.

Chop the red onions and mushrooms into small pieces and roast them on the prepared baking sheet for 10-15 minutes or until they are soft and lightly browned.

Cut the rye bread into small cubes and place in a large bowl.

Drain and rinse the black beans and add them to the bowl with the bread cubes.

Grate the Cheddar cheese and add it to the bowl with the bread and beans.

Add the roasted onions and mushrooms to the bowl, along with 2 teaspoons of ground coriander.

Mash the mixture together using a fork or potato masher, until it forms a sticky, cohesive mixture.

Divide the mixture into 4 portions and form each portion into a patty.

Place the patties on the prepared baking sheet and bake in the preheated oven for 15-20 minutes, or until they are firm and crispy.

While the burgers are baking, slice the soft rolls and halve the cherry tomatoes.

Once the burgers are cooked, assemble the sandwiches by placing a patty in each roll and topping with cherry tomato slices. Serve immediately. Enjoy!

Pasta With Roasted Tomatoes And Garlic

Ingredients

1 tablespoon kosher salt
8 ounces uncooked spaghetti
¼ cup extra-virgin olive oil, divided
2 pints multicolored cherry tomatoes
4 garlic cloves, thinly sliced
½ teaspoon kosher salt
¼ teaspoon freshly ground black pepper
2 ounces Parmigiano-Reggiano cheese, shaved
¼ cup small basil leaves

Turn a regular pasta dinner into something special with this delicious and healthy dish of pasta with roasted tomatoes and garlic. The combination of colors, flavors, and textures will make it an appealing meal for kids.

To make this dish, you'll need the following ingredients: 1 tablespoon kosher salt, 8 ounces uncooked spaghetti, ¼ cup extra-virgin olive oil (divided), 2 pints multicolored cherry tomatoes, 4 garlic cloves (thinly sliced), ½ teaspoon kosher salt, ¼ teaspoon freshly ground black pepper, 2 ounces Parmigiano-Reggiano cheese (shaved), and ¼ cup small basil leaves.

To start, preheat the oven to 425°F. Place the tomatoes in a single layer on a baking sheet and sprinkle with 1 tablespoon of olive oil, the sliced garlic, ½ teaspoon kosher salt, and ¼ teaspoon freshly ground black pepper. Roast for 25 minutes until the tomatoes are lightly charred and beginning to burst open.

While the tomatoes are roasting, bring a large pot of salted water to a boil and cook the spaghetti according to package directions.

When the pasta is cooked, drain it and add the remaining olive oil. Mix in the roasted tomatoes and garlic, Parmigiano-Reggiano cheese, and fresh basil leaves. Serve hot or at room temperature for an easy and delicious meal that the kids will love. Enjoy!

www.ingramcontent.com/pod-product-compliance
Lightning Source LLC
Chambersburg PA
CBHW041151110526
44590CB00027B/4193